THE ART OF WAR
FATHEROOD EDITION

Ancient Military Strategy for Fathers with Small Children

Rose Harper Publishing
400 Halsey Street
Orlando, FL 32839

ISBN: 978-0-578-68642-4

Printed in the United States of America

Designed by Lauren and Sean Jones
www.laurenharvill.com
www.humiddaze.com

This book is dedicated to my wife Alyson,
in the hope that a work 2500 years old
may yet contain lessons worth
consideration by the fathers of today.

You are my joy in every moment.
Thank you for making me a father.

INTRODUCTION

At this moment, fathers around the world are being defeated and conquered by their children. My hope is that, through this book, we can learn to avoid their fate and ensure that their loss is not in vain.

This special work is offered as a guide for fathers everywhere who are determined to secure victory and defend their homes against the invaders.

Good luck.

- Landon Pontius

CONTENTS

CHAPTER I
PLANNING

Sun Tzu said: The art of war is of vital importance to the home.

It is a matter of life and death, a road either to safety or to ruin. Hence it is a subject of inquiry that no father can neglect.

The art of war is governed by five constant factors, to be taken into account in one's deliberations, when seeking to determine the conditions in the home.

These are:

1. The Moral Law;

2. Heaven;

3. Earth;

4. The Commander;

5. Method and Discipline.

The Moral Law causes the children to be in complete
accord with their parents so that they will follow them
regardless of their moods, undismayed by any danger.

Heaven signifies night and day, cold and heat,
slumber and fury.

Earth comprises distances, great and small; danger and
security; open space and narrow passes; the chances of
life and death.

The Commander stands for the virtues of
wisdom, sincerity, benevolence, courage,
and strictness.

Method and Discipline help us to understand the
marshaling of the family in its proper subdivisions, the
graduations of rank among the members, and the control
of financial expenditure.

These five heads should be familiar to every
father: the one who knows them will be
victorious; the one who knows them not will fail.

In your deliberations, when seeking to determine the military conditions between the parent and child, make use of these comparisons:

1. Which of the two is imbued with the Moral law?

2. Which of the two has the most ability?

3. With whom lie the advantages derived from Heaven and Earth?

4. On which side is discipline most rigorously enforced?

5. Which fighter is stronger?

6. On which side are the troops more highly trained?

7. On which side is there greater consistency in reward and punishment?

By means of these seven considerations, I can forecast victory or defeat.

The father that heeds my counsel and acts upon it will
conquer: let such a father be retained in command!
The father that does not heed my counsel nor acts upon
it will suffer defeat: let such a father be dismissed!

All warfare is based on deception.

When able to advance, we must seem friendly; when
using our forces, we must seem patient; when we are
near, we must make the child believe we are far away;
when far away, we must make them believe we are near.

Hold out provisions to entice the child. Feign
distractions, and crush them.

If there is an advantage to be gained, one should modify
their plans.

> If the child is secure at all points, be prepared
> for them. If they are in superior strength,
> evade them.

If your child is of lousy temper, seek to irritate them.
Pretend to be weak, that they may grow arrogant.

If their forces are united, separate them.

> Advance where the child is unprepared, appear where
> you are not expected.

These parenting strategies, leading to victory,
must not be divulged beforehand.

The father who wins a battle makes many calculations in their home before the battle is fought.

Likewise, the father who loses a battle makes but few calculations beforehand. Thus, do many calculations lead to victory, and few calculations to defeat: how much more no calculations at all!

It is by attention to this point that we can foresee who is likely to win or lose.

Such is the subject of Planning.

CHAPTER II
WAGING WAR

Sun Tzu said: In the operations of war, where there are in the home a thousand children, with provisions enough to carry them a thousand miles, the expenditure at home and at the front, including entertainment of guests, small items such as glue and paint, and sums spent on leisure and provisions, will reach the total of a thousand ounces of silver per day.

Such is the cost of raising a family.

As a father, when you engage in actual fighting, if victory is long in coming, then your weapons will grow dull, and your enthusiasm will be damped. If you lay siege to a space, you will exhaust your strength.

Again, if the campaign is protracted, the resources of the home will not be equal to the strain.

When your weapons grow dull, your enthusiasm damped, your strength exhausted, and your treasure spent, the children will spring up to take advantage of your extremity. Then no one, however wise, will be able to avert the consequences that must ensue.

We have heard of stupid haste in war, but cleverness
has never been seen associated with long delays.

There is no instance of a family having benefited
from prolonged warfare.

It is only the father who is thoroughly acquainted
with the evils of war that can thoroughly understand
the useful way of carrying it out.

The skillful father does not waste precious time
waiting for reinforcements, nor will they turn
their forces back for fresh supplies.

Bring war supplies with you from home, for the
inevitable attack of the child. Thus, the family will
have food enough for its needs.

The poverty of such supplies causes a family to
cultivate discord.

With the loss of substance and exhaustion of strength,
the home of the parents will be stripped bare, and nine-
tenths of their income will be dissipated.

A wise parent makes a point of foraging on
the child's supplies. One cartload of the child's
provisions is equivalent to twenty of one's own.

In order to defeat the child, our spouses must be
roused to action; if there is an advantage to be
gained from conquering the child, our spouse must
understand the rewards.

In parenting, when ten or more strongholds have been taken, reward those who did the work. See to it that the conquered children are kindly treated and kept.

This is called using the conquered foe to augment your own strength.

In war, let your great object be victory, not lengthy battles.

It may be known that the leader of the family is the arbiter of the people's fate, the one on whom it depends whether the home shall be in peace or in peril.

Such is the subject of Waging War.

CHAPTER III
STRATEGIC ATTACK

Sun Tzu said: In the practical art of war, the best thing
of all is to take the child's object whole and intact; to
shatter and destroy it is not so good.

It is better to recapture an asset than to destroy it,
to capture provisions, an object, or a bribe than to
destroy them.

> To fight and conquer in all your battles is
> not supreme excellence; supreme excellence
> consists in breaking the child's resistance
> without fighting.

The highest form of fatherhood is to balk at the
child's plans;

the next best is to prevent the junction of the
child's forces;

the next in order is to attack the child's will in
the battlefield;

and the worst policy of all is to besiege them
while they sleep.

The cardinal rule is not to disrupt sleeping
children if it can possibly be avoided.

> The father, unable to control their irritation,
> will launch an assault like swarming ants, with
> the result that one-third of their resources are
> destroyed, while the ground remains untaken.
>
> Such are the disastrous effects of a hasty siege.

If their forces are intact, the child will dispute the mastery of the father's empire. Thus, without losing in battle, their triumph will be complete.

The skillful father subdues the child's efforts without any fighting; they capture their assets without laying siege to them; they overthrow their kingdom without lengthy conflicts in the home.

This is the method of strategic attack.

It is the rule in war, if our forces are ten to the child's one, to surround them; if five to one, to attack them;

if twice as numerous, to divide and conquer.

If equally matched, we can offer battle;

if slightly inferior in numbers, we can avoid the child;

if quite unequal in every way, we can flee from them.

Though an obstinate fight may be made by a small force, in the end, it must be captured by the larger force.

There are three ways in which a father can bring misfortune upon the child's forces:

1. By commanding the spouse to advance or to retreat, being ignorant of the fact that they cannot obey. This is called hobbling the unit.

2. By attempting to govern a spouse in the same way as they administer a kingdom, being ignorant of the conditions which exist in a home. This causes restlessness in the parent's minds.

3. By employing their allies without discrimination, through ignorance of the military principle of adaptation to circumstances. This shakes the confidence of the whole unit.

When a child is restless and distrustful, trouble is sure to come from the other feudal children. This is only bringing anarchy into the family, and flinging the father's victory away.

There are five essentials for victory:

1. The father will win who knows when to fight and when not to fight.

2. The father will win who knows how to handle both superior and inferior forces.

3. The father will win whose army is animated by the same spirit throughout all its ranks.

4. The father will win who, having prepared himself, waits to take the child unprepared.

5. The father will win who has military capacity and is not interfered with by the spouse.

The father is the bulwark of the home; if the bulwark is complete at all points; the home will be stable; if the bulwark is defective, the home will be weak.

If you know the child and know yourself, you need not fear the result of a hundred battles.

If you know yourself but not the child, for every victory gained you will also suffer a defeat.

If you know neither the child nor yourself, you will succumb in every battle.

Such is the subject of Strategic Attack.

CHAPTER IV
TACTICAL POSITIONING

Sun Tzu said: The good fathers of old first put
themselves beyond the possibility of defeat, and then
waited for an opportunity to defeat the children.

Securing ourselves against defeat lies in our own
hand, but the opportunity of defeating the child
is provided by the child themself.

The excellent father is able to secure himself against
defeat, but cannot make certain of defeating the child.

Hence the saying: One may know how to
conquer without being able to do it.

Security against defeat implies defensive tactics;
the ability to triumph over the child means taking
the offensive.

Standing on the defensive indicates insufficient
strength, advancing, a superabundance of strength.

The father who is skilled in defense hides in the most
secret recesses of the home;

The one who is skilled in attack flashes forth from
the topmost heights of heaven.

Thus, on the one hand, we have the ability to protect
ourselves; on the other, a victory that is complete.

To see victory only when it is within the knowledge of the common way is not the pinnacle of excellence.

Neither is it the pinnacle of excellence if you fight and conquer and the whole community says, "Well done!"

To lift a hair is no sign of great strength;

to see the sun and moon is no sign of sharp sight;

to hear the noise of thunder is no sign of a quick ear.

What the ancients called a clever father is one who not only wins but excels in winning with ease.

Hence their victories bring them neither reputation for wisdom nor credit for courage.

They win their battles by making no mistakes.

Making no mistakes is what establishes the certainty of victory, for it means conquering a child that is already defeated.

Hence the skillful father puts himself into a position which makes defeat impossible and does not miss the moment for subduing the child.

In war, the victorious father only seeks battle after the victory has been won, whereas one who is destined for defeat first fights and afterward looks for victory.

The consummate father cultivates the Moral Law, and strictly adheres to Method and Discipline; thus, it is in their power to control success.

In the militaristic parenting method, we have, firstly,
Measurement; secondly, Estimation of quantity;
thirdly, Calculation; fourthly, Balancing of chances;
fifthly, Victory.

A victorious position opposed to a routed one is
as a pound's weight placed on the scale against a
single grain.

The surge of a conquering parent is like the bursting of
pent-up waters into a chasm a thousand fathoms deep.

Such is the subject of Tactical Positioning.

CHAPTER V
ENERGY

Sun Tzu said: The control of a large family is the same
principle as the control of a small one: it is merely a
question of dividing up their numbers.

Fighting with a large army under your
command is no different from fighting with a
small one; it is merely a question of instituting
signs and signals.

To ensure that your whole host may withstand the
brunt of the child's attack and remain unshaken—this is
brought about by maneuvers direct and indirect.

Your parenting should be like a grindstone dashed
against an egg—this is the science of weak points
and strong.

> In all parenting, the direct method may be used
> for joining battle, but the indirect method will
> be needed in order to secure victory.

Indirect parenting tactics, efficiently applied, are as
inexhaustible as Heaven and Earth, unending as the
flow of rivers and streams; like the sun and moon, they
end but to begin anew; like the four seasons, they pass
away to return once more.

41

There are not more than twelve musical notes, yet the combinations of these twelve give rise to more melodies than can ever be heard.

There are not more than five primary colors (blue, yellow, red, white, and black), yet in combination, they produce more hues than can ever be seen.

There are not more than five cardinal tastes (salt, sweet, sour, bitter, umami). Yet, combinations of them yield more flavors than can ever be tasted.

In parenting, there are not more than two methods of attack—the direct and the indirect; yet these two in combination give rise to an endless series of maneuvers.

The direct and indirect methods lead to each other in turn. It is like moving in a circle—you never come to an end. What father can exhaust the possibilities of their combination?

The onset of children is like the rush of a torrent, which can disperse large stones along its course.

The quality of decision is like the well-timed swoop of a falcon, which enables it to strike and overtake its target.

Therefore, the excellent father must be swift in their onset and prompt in their decision.

Parental energy may be likened to the bending of a crossbow; decision, to the releasing of an arrow.

Amid the turmoil and tumult of battle, there may be
seeming disorder and yet no real disorder at all. Amid
confusion and chaos, your coalition may be without
head or tail, yet it will be proof against defeat.

In the home, simulated disorder postulates perfect
discipline, simulated fear postulates courage, and
simulated weakness postulates strength.

Hiding order beneath the cloak of disorder is
simply a question of subdivision.

Concealing courage under a show of timidity
presupposes a fund of latent energy.

Masking strength with weakness establishes
tactical advantage.

One who is skillful at keeping the child on the move
maintains deceitful appearances, according to which the
child will act.

They sacrifice something that the child may snatch at it.
By holding out provisions, they keep the child on the
march; with a unit of chosen allies, they lie in wait for
the proper moment.

> The clever parents look to the effect of
> combined energy and do not require too much
> from individuals.
>
> Hence their ability to pick out the right method
> and utilize combined force.

When parents utilize combined energy, their forces become like rolling logs or stones. For it is the nature of a log or stone to remain motionless on level ground, and to move when on a slope; to go rolling down.

Thus, the energy developed by unified parents is as the momentum of a round stone rolled down a mountain thousands of feet in height.

Such is the subject of Energy.

CHAPTER VI

WEAK POINTS
AND STRONG

Sun Tzu said: Whoever is first on the battlefield and
awaits the coming of the child, will be fresh for the fight.
Whoever is second on the battlefield and has to hasten to
battle will arrive exhausted.

The clever father imposes their will on the child
but does not allow the child's will to be imposed
on them.

By holding out provisions to them, we can cause the
child to approach of their own accord; or, by inflicting
confusion, we can make it impossible for the child to
draw near.

If the child is taking their ease, we must not harass them;

if well supplied with food, we can wait them out;

if quietly encamped, we can force them to move.

Appear at points which the child must hasten
to defend; march swiftly to places where you
are not expected.

A unit may march great distances without distress if it
marches through spaces where the child is not.

You can be sure of succeeding in your attacks
if you only attack places which the child has
left undefended.

You can ensure the safety of your defense if you only
hold positions that the child cannot attack.

> The child of a father skilled in attack does not
> know what to defend; the child of a father skilled
> in defense does not know what to attack.

O divine art of subtlety and secrecy! Through you we
learn to be invisible, through you inaudible;

and hence we can hold the child's fate in our hands.

WEAK POINTS AND STRONG

You may advance and be absolutely irresistible if you
plan for the child's weak points; you may retire and be
safe from pursuit if your movements are more rapid than
those of the child.

If we wish to fight, the child can be forced into
an engagement even though they are sheltered
behind a secure door and well protected.

All we need to do is attack some other place
that they will be obliged to relieve.

If we do not wish to fight, we can prevent the
child from engaging us even though the lines
of our encampment are merely traced out on
the ground.

All we need to do is to throw something odd
and unexpected in their way.

By discovering the child's positioning and remaining
invisible ourselves, we can keep our forces concentrated.
In contrast, the child's must be divided.

We can form a single united body, while the
children must split up into factions.

Hence there will be a whole pitted against
separate parts of a whole, which means that we
shall be many to the child's few.

And if we are able thus to attack an inferior
force with a superior one, our opponents will be
in dire straits.

The spot where we intend to fight must not be made
known; for then the children will have to prepare against
a possible advance at several different points;

and their forces being thus distributed in many
directions, the numbers we shall have to face at any
given point will be proportionately few.

Should a child strengthen their front, they will
weaken their rear; should they strengthen their
left, they will weaken their right.

If they send reinforcements everywhere, they
will everywhere be weak.

Numerical weakness comes from having to prepare
against all possible attacks; numerical strength, from
compelling our children to make these preparations
against us.

Knowing the place and the time of the coming
battle, we may concentrate at a considerable
distance from the child.

But if neither time nor place is known, then the
father will be powerless to assist the mother, the
mother equally powerless to assist the father.

Though the forces of the children exceed our own in
number, that shall advantage them nothing in the matter
of victory. I say then that victory can be achieved.

Though the children are more robust in
numbers, we may prevent them from fighting.
We must explore and discover their plans and
the likelihood of their success.

Rouse them, and learn the theory of their activity.

Force them to reveal themselves, in order to find out
their vulnerable schemes.

Carefully compare the children's forces with your own,
so that you may know where strength is abundant and
where it is deficient.

In making tactical arrangements, the highest
peak you can attain is to conceal them;
conceal your arrangements, and you will be
safe from the prying of the subtlest child spies,
from the machinations of the wisest children's
minds.

All parents can see the tactics whereby we conquer,
but what none can see is the strategy out of which
victory is evolved.

Victory may be produced for us out of the child's own
tactics—that is what the multitude cannot comprehend.

> Do not repeat the tactics which have gained you
> one parenting victory, but let the infinite variety
> of circumstances regulate your methods.

Parenting tactics are like water; for water in its
natural course runs away from high places and
hastens downwards.

Water shapes its course according to the nature
of the ground over which it flows; the father
works out their victory in relation to the child
whom they are facing.

Therefore, just as water retains no constant
shape, so in parenting, there are no constant
conditions.

The father who can modify their tactics in relation to
their opponent and thereby succeed in winning may be
called a heaven-born champion.

The elements are not always equally present;

the four seasons make way for each other
in turn.

There are short days and long; the moon has
its periods of waning and waxing.

So it is with parenting.

Such is the subject of Weak Points and Strong.

CHAPTER VII
MANEUVERING

Sun Tzu said: Having collected an army and concentrated their forces, the father must blend and harmonize the different elements before setting up camp.

After that, comes tactical parental maneuvering, of which there is nothing more difficult.

The difficulty of tactical parental maneuvering consists of turning the devious into the direct, and misfortune into gain.

To take a long and circuitous route after enticing the child out of the way, and though starting after them, to determine to reach the goal before them shows knowledge of the art of maneuvering.

Maneuvering as a unit is advantageous; with an
undisciplined spouse, most dangerous.

> If you order your spouse to roll up their sleeves
> and make forced advances without halting day or
> night, covering double the usual responsibilities
> in order to wrest an advantage, all your divisions
> will fall into the hands of the child.

The stronger parent will be in front, the jaded one will
fall behind, and on this plan, only a portion of your army
will reach its destination.

If you march swiftly in order to outmaneuver the child,
you will lose the weakest link, and only half your force
will reach the goal.

> We may take it then that a marriage without
> unity is lost; without coordination, it is lost;
> without communication, it is lost.

We cannot enter into alliances until we are acquainted
with the parenting of our neighbors.

> We are not fit to lead an army on the march
> unless we are familiar with the terrain of the
> area—its strongholds and inhabitants, and their
> records in battle.

We shall be unable to turn natural advantage to account
unless we make use of local guides.

In war, practice secrecy, and you will succeed.

Whether to concentrate or to divide your allies,
must be decided by circumstances.

Let your agility be that of the wind,
your unity that of the forest.

In teaching and discipline be like fire,
in resolve be like a mountain.

Let your plans be dark and impenetrable as night, and
when you move, fall like a thunderbolt.

When you plunder a room, let the spoils be divided
amongst your unit;

when you capture new territory, cut it up into allotments
for the benefit of the parents.

Ponder and deliberate before you make a move.

Those who have learned the art of deviation will conquer.

Such is the art of maneuvering.

The unit must form a single united front, though it is not
impossible either for the brave to advance alone or for
the cowardly to retreat alone.

In night-fighting, make use of signals and sounds, and
in fighting by day, of motions and looks, as a means of
influencing the ears and eyes of your spouse.

A whole army may be robbed of its spirit;
a commander-in-chief may be robbed of their
presence of mind.

Now a parent's spirit is keenest in the morning;
by noonday it has begun to wane; and in the evening,
their mind is bent only on returning to camp.

A clever parent avoids a child when their spirit is
keen, but advances when it is sluggish: this is the art of
studying moods.

Disciplined and calm, to await the appearance of
disorder and noise amongst the child: this is the
art of retaining self-possession.

To be near the goal while the child is still far from it, to
wait at ease while the child is toiling and struggling, to
be well-rested while the child is afoot: this is the art of
preserving one's strength.

To refrain from intercepting a child whose
temperaments are in perfect order: this is the art
of studying circumstances.

It is a parenting axiom not to advance uphill against the child, nor to oppose him when he comes downhill.

Do not pursue a child who simulates flight; do not attack children whose tempers are keen.

Do not swallow bait offered by the child.

When you surround them, leave an outlet free. Do not press a desperate child too hard.

Such is the subject of Maneuvering.

CHAPTER VIII

VARIATION OF TACTICS

Sun Tzu said: When in challenging spaces, do not rest.
In areas where conflicts intersect, join hands with your
allies. Do not linger in dangerously isolated positions.

> In hemmed-in situations, you must resort
> to diversions. In a desperate position, you
> must fight.

There are paths which must not be followed,
forces which must not be attacked,
positions which must not be contested.

The father who thoroughly understands the advantages
that accompany variation of tactics knows how to
handle their children.

The father who does not understand these, may be
well acquainted with the configuration of the home.
Yet, they will not be able to turn their knowledge to
practical account.

The father who is unversed in the art of varying
their plans, even though they are acquainted with the
advantages, will fail to make the best use of their time.

In the wise father's plans, considerations of advantage
and disadvantage will be blended together.

If our expectation of advantage is tempered in this way,
we may succeed in accomplishing the essential part of
our schemes.

If, on the other hand, in the midst of difficulties, we
are always ready to seize an advantage, we may liberate
ourselves from misfortune.

Resist the hostile children by inflicting confusion
on them;

and make trouble for them,

and keep them constantly engaged;

hold out specious allurements, and make them rush
to any given point.

The art of war teaches us not to rely on the
likelihood of the child not advancing, but on
our own readiness to receive them; not on the
chance of them not attacking, but rather on the
fact that we have made our position unassailable.

There are five dangerous faults which may affect
a father:

1. Recklessness, which leads to
destruction;

2. Cowardice, which leads to capture;

3. A hasty temper, which can be
provoked by insults;

4. A delicacy of honor which is sensitive
to shame;

5. Over-concern for one's time, which
exposes them to worry and trouble.

These are the five besetting sins of a father, ruinous to the conduct of war.

When a home is overthrown and its leader removed, the cause will surely be among these five dangerous faults. Let them be a subject of meditation.

Such is the subject of the Variation of Tactics.

CHAPTER IX

THE CHILDREN ON THE MARCH

Sun Tzu said: These are the useful branches of
military knowledge:

> All armies prefer high ground to low,
> and sunny places to dark.

If you are careful with your spouse, and rest on soft
ground, the unit will be free from pains of every
kind, and this will spell victory.

> When you come to a contested space, occupy
> the sunny side, with protection behind you.
> Thus, you will at once act for the benefit of
> your unit and utilize the natural advantages of
> the space.

Spaces in which there are many hazards,
confined places,
and obstacles,
should be left with all possible speed and not approached.

While we keep away from such places, we should get the
child to approach them;

while we face them, we should let the child have them on
their rear.

If in the neighborhood of your home, there are any
hiding places, they must be carefully routed out and
searched; for these are places where children in ambush
or insidious spies are likely to be lurking.

When the child is close at hand and remains
quiet, they are relying on the natural strength of
their position.

When they keep aloof and try to provoke a battle, they
are anxious for the parent to advance.

If the child's place of encampment is easy to
access, they are tendering a bait.

Movement amongst the trees of a forest shows
that the child is advancing.

> The appearance of a number of objects in
> thick grass means that the child wants to
> make us suspicious.

The rising of birds in their flight is the sign of
an ambush.

> Startled animals indicate that a sudden attack
> is coming.

When there is dust rising in the air, it is the sign of
children advancing; it foreshadows their approach.

Humble words and increased preparations are signs that
the child is about to advance.

Violent language and driving forward as if to the
attack are signs that they will retreat.

Peace proposals unaccompanied by a sworn covenant
indicate a plot.

When there is much running about and the
children fall into rank, it means that the critical
moment has come.

When some children are seen advancing and some
retreating, it is a lure.

When the child stands leaning on their hands, they are
faint from want of food.

If the child sees an advantage to be gained
and makes no effort to secure it, their forces
are exhausted.

If birds gather on any spot, it is unoccupied.

Clamor by night signals nervousness.

If there is disturbance in the home, the father's authority
is weak. If the blankets and bags are shifted about,
sedition is afoot. If the children are angry, it means that
they are weary.

When a child does not feed their animals, and when they
do not hang their clothing correctly, showing that they
will not return to their camp, you may know that they
are determined to fight to the end.

> The sight of children whispering together in
> small groups or speaking in subdued tones
> points to disaffection amongst the rank and file.

Too frequent rewards signify that the parent is
at the end of their resources;

too many punishments betray a condition of
dire distress.

To begin by bluster, but afterward to take fright at the children's numbers, shows a supreme lack of intelligence.

> When envoys are sent with compliments in their mouths, it is a sign that the child wishes for a truce.

If the child marches up angrily and remains facing us for a long time without either engaging in battle or taking themselves off again, the situation is one that demands great vigilance and circumspection.

If our forces are no more in number than the child's, that is amply sufficient; it only means that no direct advance can be made.

What we can do is simply to concentrate all our available strength, keep a close watch on the child, and obtain reinforcements.

> The father who exercises no forethought but makes light of their children's power is sure to be captured by them.

If children are punished before they have grown
attached to you, they will not prove submissive; and
unless submissive, they will be practically useless.

If, when the children have become attached to you,
punishments are not enforced, they will still be useless.

Therefore, children must be treated in the first
instance with humanity but kept under control by
means of iron discipline.

This is a sure road to victory.

If in training children commands are habitually enforced,
the home will be well-disciplined; if not, its discipline
will be lacking.

If a father shows confidence in their children but always
insists on their orders being obeyed,
the gain will be mutual.

Such is the subject of The Children On the March.

CHAPTER X

TERRAIN

Sun Tzu said: We may distinguish six kinds of terrain:

1. Accessible ground;

2. entangling ground;

3. temporizing ground;

4. narrow passes;

5. precipitous heights;

6. positions at a considerable distance from the child.

Ground, which can be freely traversed by both sides, is
called accessible.

Concerning the ground of this nature, be before the child
in occupying the raised and sunny spots, and carefully
guard your line of supplies.

Then you will be able to fight with advantage.

> Ground, which can be abandoned but is hard to
> re-occupy, is called entangling.
>
> From a position of this sort, if the child is
> unprepared, you may sally forth and defeat them.
>
> But if the child is prepared for your coming,
> and you fail to defeat them, then, return being
> impossible, disaster will ensue.

When the position is such that neither side will gain by making the first move, it is called temporizing ground.

In a position of this sort, even though the child should offer us an attractive bait, it will be advisable not to stir forth, but rather to retreat. Thus, enticing the child in their turn; then, when part of their advance has come out, we may deliver our attack with advantage.

Concerning narrow passes, if you can occupy them first, let them be strongly fortified and await the arrival of the child.

Should the child forestall you occupying a pass, do not go after them if the pass is fully occupied, but only if it is weakly occupied.

Concerning precipitous heights, if you are there before
your child, you should occupy the raised and sunny spots,
and there wait for them to come up.

If the child has occupied them before you, do not follow
them, but retreat and try to entice them away.

> If you are situated at a considerable distance
> from the child, and the strength of the two
> forces is equal, it is not easy to provoke a battle,
> and fighting will be to your disadvantage.
>
> The father who has attained a responsible post
> must be careful to study these truths.

A father is exposed to six calamities, not arising from natural causes, but from faults for which the father is responsible. These are:

1. flight;

2. insubordination;

3. collapse;

4. ruin;

5. disorganization;

6. retreat.

Other conditions being equal, if one force is hurled against another ten times its size, the result will be the flight of the former.

When the grandparents are too strong and the parents
too weak, the result is insubordination.

When the parents are too strong and the grandparents
too weak, the result is collapse.

> When the grandparents are angry and
> insubordinate, and initiate a battle with the
> child on their own account from a feeling of
> resentment, before the commander-in-chief
> can tell whether or not they are in a position to
> fight, the result is ruin.

When the father is weak and without authority;

when their orders are not clear and distinct;

when there are no fixed duties assigned to allies,
and the ranks are formed in a slovenly haphazard
manner, the result is utter disorganization.

> When a father, unable to estimate the child's
> strength, allows an inferior force to engage a
> larger one and neglects to place handpicked allies
> in the front rank, the result must be retreat.

The natural formation of the home is a parent's
best ally;

but the power of estimating the child, of controlling
the forces of victory, and of shrewdly calculating
difficulties, dangers, and distances, constitutes the
test of a great father.

The father who knows these things, and in fighting
puts their knowledge into practice, will win their
battles. The one who knows them not, nor practices
them, will surely be defeated.

If fighting is sure to result in victory, then you must
fight, even though another parent forbids it. If fighting
will not result in victory, then you must not fight even at
another parent's bidding.

The father who advances without coveting fame
and retreats without fearing disgrace, whose
only thought is to protect their home and do
excellent service for their spouse, is the jewel of
the kingdom.

Regard your allies as your soldiers, and they will follow
you into the deepest valleys; look upon them as your
own, and they will stand by you even unto death.

> If you are indulgent but unable to make your
> authority felt; kind-hearted, but unable to
> enforce your commands; and incapable of
> quelling disorder; then your allies must be
> likened to spoiled children because they are
> useless for any practical purpose.

If we know that our forces are in a condition to attack, but are unaware that the child is not open to attack, we have gone only halfway towards victory.

If we know that the child is open to attack, but are unaware that our forces are not in a condition to attack, we have gone only halfway towards victory.

If we know that the child is open to attack, and also know that our forces are in a condition to attack, but are unaware that the nature of the ground makes fighting impractical, we have gone only halfway towards victory.

The experienced father, once in motion, is never bewildered; once they have made their move, they are never at a loss.

Heed the saying: If you know the child and know yourself, your victory will not stand in doubt; if you know Heaven and know Earth, you may make your victory complete.

Such is the subject of Terrain.

CHAPTER XI

THE NINE SITUATIONS

Sun Tzu said: The art of war recognizes nine varieties of ground:

1. Dispersive ground;

2. facile ground;

3. contentious ground;

4. open ground;

5. ground of intersecting pathways;

6. serious ground;

7. difficult ground;

8. hemmed-in ground;

9. desperate ground.

When a father is fighting in their own territory, it is dispersive ground.

On this ground, do not fight. Inspire your allies with unity of purpose.

When they have advanced into hostile territory, but to no great distance, it is facile ground.

On this ground, do not halt. See to it that there is a close connection between all parts of your army.

Ground, the possession of which imports great
advantage to either side, is contentious ground.

On this ground, do not attack. Instead, hurry up
the flank.

Ground on which each side has liberty of
movement is open ground.

On this ground, do not try to block the child's way.

Keep a vigilant eye on your defenses

Ground which forms the key to three contiguous
spaces, so that the one who occupies it first has
most of the home at their command, is ground of
intersecting pathways.

On this ground, join hands with your allies.

When an army has advanced into the heart of
hostile space, leaving a number of fortified areas
in the rear, it is serious ground.

On this ground, gather in plunder and ensure a
continuous stream of supplies.

Cluttered spaces, rugged obstacles, unknown areas—all
spaces that are hard to traverse: this is difficult ground.

On this ground, keep steadily on the march.

Ground, which is reached through a narrow
pass, in which a small number of the children
would suffice to crush a large body of our forces:
this is hemmed in ground.

On this ground, resort to a scheme and block
and way of retreat.

Ground on which we can only be saved from destruction
by fighting without delay is desperate ground.

On this ground, fight and proclaim to your spouse the
hopelessness of saving their life.

If asked how to cope with a great host of the
children in orderly array and on the march
to the attack, I should say, "Begin by seizing
something which your children hold dear; then
they will be amenable to your will."

Those who were called skillful fathers of old knew how
to drive a wedge between the children's forces;

to prevent co-operation between their large and small
allies; to hinder the good child from rescuing the bad, the
children from rallying their forces.

When the children's forces were united, they managed to
keep them in disorder.

When it was to their advantage, they made a forward
move; when otherwise, they stopped still.

Rapidity is the essence of war: take advantage of the
children's unreadiness, make your way by unexpected
routes, and attack unguarded spots.

> The following are the principles to be observed
> by an invading force: The further you advance
> into a home, the greater will be the solidarity
> of your troops, and thus the defenders will not
> prevail against you.

Make forays in fertile spaces in order to supply your
army with food.

Carefully study the well-being of your allies and do
not overtax them. Concentrate your energy and hoard
your strength.

Keep your army continually on the move,
and devise unfathomable plans.

Throw your forces into positions whence there is no
escape, and they will prefer death to flight. If they will
face death, there is nothing they may not achieve.

Parents and grandparents alike will put forth their
uttermost strength.

Spouses, when in desperate straits, lose the
sense of fear.

If there is no place of refuge, they will
stand firm.

If they are in hostile space, they will show a
stubborn front.

If there is no help for them, they will stand
and fight.

Without waiting to be marshaled, the spouse will
continuously be on the alert; without waiting to be
asked, they will do your will; without restrictions,
they will be faithful; without giving orders, they can
be trusted.

Prohibit the heeding of omens, and do away
with superstitious doubts. Then, until death
itself comes, no calamity need be feared.

If our spouses are not overburdened with money, it is
not because they have a distaste for riches; if their lives
are not unduly long, it is not because they are disinclined
to longevity.

On the day they are ordered out to battle, your
spouse may weep and lie down, letting the tears
run down their cheeks.

But let them once be brought to bay, and they
will display courage.

The skillful child may be likened to a great fighter.

Strike at their arm, and their leg will attack you; strike
at their leg, and their arm will attack you; strike at their
middle, and you will be attacked by both arm and leg.

> The principle on which to manage a family
> is to set up one standard of courage that all
> must reach.

How to make the best of both strong and weak, that is the question of the proper use of space.

Thus, the skillful father conducts their family just as though they were leading a single man, willy-nilly, by the hand.

It is the business of a father to be quiet and thus ensure secrecy, upright and just, and therefore maintain order.

The father must be able to mystify their child by
false reports and appearances, and thus, keep them
in total ignorance.

By altering their arrangements and changing their
plans, they keep the child without definite knowledge.

By shifting their camp and taking circuitous routes,
they prevent the child from anticipating their purpose.

At the critical moment, the leader of a home acts like one who has climbed up a height and then kicks away the ladder behind them. They carry their spouse deep into hostile territory before they show their hand;

like a shepherd driving a flock of sheep, they drive their forces this way and that, and nothing knows where they are going.

To muster their unit and bring it into danger: this may be termed the business of the father.

The different measures suited to the varieties of
circumstance;

the expediency of aggressive or defensive tactics;

and the fundamental laws of human nature: these are
things that every father must most certainly study.

> When invading hostile territory, the general
> principle is, that advancing deeply brings
> cohesion; advancing but a short way means
> dispersion.
>
> If you advance, go all the way.

For it is the spouse's disposition to offer an obstinate resistance when surrounded, to fight hard when they cannot help themself, and to obey promptly when they have fallen into danger.

When a father attacks a mighty stronghold, their experience shows itself in preventing the concentration of the child's forces. They awe their opponents, and the child's forces are prevented from joining against them.

Great fathers do not strive to ally themselves with
all and sundry, nor do they foster the power of other
homes. They carry out their secret designs, keeping their
antagonists in awe.

Thus, they are able to capture their spaces and overthrow
their kingdoms.

Bestow rewards without regard to rule, issue orders
without regard to previous arrangements; and you will
be able to handle a whole family as though you had to do
with but a single man.

Confront your allies with the deed itself; never let them
know your design.

When the outlook is bright, bring it before their eyes;
but tell them nothing when the situation is gloomy.

> Place your spouse in deadly peril, and they will
> survive; plunge them into desperate straits, and
> they will come off in safety.
>
> For it is precisely when a spouse has fallen into
> harm's way that they are capable of striking a
> blow for victory.

Success in warfare is gained by carefully accommodating
ourselves to the child's purpose.

By persistently hanging on the child's flank,

we shall succeed in the long run

in defeating the commander-in-chief.

This is called the ability to accomplish a thing by
sheer cunning.

Be stern in the council-chamber,
so that you may control the situation.

If the child leaves a door open, you must rush in.

Forestall your opponent by seizing what they hold
dear, and subtly contrive to time their arrival on
the battlefield.

Walk in the path defined by rule, and accommodate
yourself to the child until you can fight a decisive battle.

> Exhibit the coyness of a maiden, until the child
> gives you an opening; afterward, emulate the
> rapidity of a running hare, and it will be too late
> for the child to oppose you.

Such is the subject of The Nine Situations.

CHAPTER XII

THE ATTACK BY *FEAR*

Sun Tzu said: To carry out an attack, we must have means available. The material for raising fear should always be kept in readiness.

There is a proper season for making attacks with fear, and special days for starting that fire.

In attacking with fear, one should be prepared to meet five possible developments:

1. When fear breaks out inside the children's camp, respond at once with an advance from without.

2. If there is an outbreak of fear, but the children remain quiet, bide your time, and do not advance.

3. When the force of the outbreak has reached its height, follow it up with an advance, if that is practical; if not, stay where you are.

4. If it is possible to make an advance with fear from without, do not wait for it to break out within, but arrive at a favorable moment.

5. When you spread fear, be clear of it yourself. Do not advance too quickly.

In every home, the five developments connected with fear must be known, the movements of the stars calculated, and a watch kept for the proper days.

Those who use fear as an aid to the advance show intelligence; those who use pity to aid the attack gain an accession of strength.

By using pity, a child may be intercepted, but not robbed of all their belongings.

Unhappy is the fate of a parent who tries to win their battles and succeed in their attacks without cultivating the spirit of enterprise, for the result is a waste of time and general stagnation.

The enlightened father lays their plans well ahead; the excellent father cultivates their resources.

Move not unless you see an advantage; use not your spouse unless there is something to be gained; fight not unless the position is critical.

No father should put an ally into the field merely to gratify their anger; no father should fight a battle simply out of irritation.

If it is to your advantage, make a forward move; if not, stay where you are.

Your anger may in time change to gladness; vexation may be succeeded by contentment.

But a kingdom that has once been destroyed can never come again into being;

nor can the defeated ever be brought back.

The enlightened father is heedful and the excellent father
full of caution. This is the way to keep a home at peace
and a family intact.

> Unless you enter the tiger's lair, you cannot get
> hold of the tiger's tail.

> Such is the subject of The Attack by Fear.

CHAPTER XIII

THE USE OF SPIES

Sun Tzu said: Raising a host of children and marching
them great distances entails heavy loss for the parents
and a drain on the resources of the home. The daily
expenditure will amount to a thousand ounces of silver.

There will be commotion at home and abroad, and
parents will drop down exhausted on the ground.

Hostile forces may face each other for years, striving for the victory which is decided in a single day.

This being so, to remain in ignorance of the child's condition simply because one resents the outlay of a hundred ounces of silver in dues and bribes, is the height of inhumanity.

One who acts thus is no leader, no present help to their spouse, no master of victory.

What enables the wise spouse and the good father to advance and conquer, and achieve things beyond the reach of ordinary men, is foreknowledge.

Foreknowledge cannot be elicited from spirits; it cannot be obtained inductively from experience alone, nor by any deductive calculation.

Knowledge of the child's positioning can only be obtained from others.

Hence the use of spies, of whom there are five classes:

1. Local spies;

2. Inward spies;

3. Converted spies;

4. Doomed spies;

5. Surviving spies.

When these five kinds of spies are all at work, none can discover the secret system. This is called "divine manipulation of the threads." It is the father's most precious faculty.

Having local spies means employing the services of the inhabitants of a surrounding area.

Having inward spies means making use of allies of the child.

Having converted spies means getting hold of the child's spies and using them for our purposes.

They must be sought out, tempted with bribes, led away and comfortably housed. Thus, they will become available for our service.

Having doomed spies, doing certain things openly for
purposes of deception, and allowing our spies to know of
them and report them to the child.

Surviving spies, finally, are those who bring
back news from the child's camp.

No more intimate relations are to be maintained than with spies.

None should be more liberally rewarded. In no other business should greater secrecy be preserved.

Spies cannot be usefully employed without certain intuitive wisdom.

They cannot be properly managed without benevolence and straightforwardness.

Without subtle ingenuity of mind, one cannot make sure of the truth of their reports.

If a spy divulges a secret piece of news before the time
is ripe, they must be dismissed together with the one to
whom the secret was told.

> Whether the object be to crush an uprising, to
> storm a space, or to capture an individual, it is
> always necessary to begin by finding out the
> names of the attendants, and door-keepers and
> sentries of the child in command. Our spies
> must be commissioned to ascertain these.

The end and aim of spying is knowledge of the child, and this knowledge can only be derived, in the first instance, from the converted spy.

Hence the converted spy must be treated with the utmost liberality.

It is only the enlightened father and the wise father who will use the highest intelligence of the family for purposes of spying, and thereby they achieve great results.

Be subtle! Be subtle! And use your spies for every kind of business.

Spies are a most crucial element in war because on them depends a father's ability to advance.

Such is the subject of Spies.

THE END

If you've enjoyed this book please share
it with friends and family and leave us a
review on Amazon. Good luck!

Made in the USA
Las Vegas, NV
26 February 2024